JOURNEY BACK TO
ZANZIBAR

Monica D. Brown

Dedication

I dedicate this book to: my father, the late Gersham Elkanah Brown, a born people builder, poet and patriot, Iciline Brown, my beloved mother with whom I still play cricket, my entire family and my unnamed ancestors, 'whose whispered wisdom guides me still'.

Contents

Acknowledgments

I would like to thank God for my family, the strong, loving circle you are. Mom, thanks for your help in editing the poems when you were in the U.K. Johann, my son, thanks for your patience and understanding and for being our official photographer. You were such a great part of that journey we made in August 2009. My brother Noel! What a staggering experience we all shared, discovering the gritty reality and glory of Tanzania and Zanzibar. Thank you for your leadership and wisdom.

Thanks to the BBC for choosing me to be one of its participants in the 2007 series, "Who am I?" Four generations of our family were represented in the final 25 minute radio documentary aired on the BBC regional network. Elonka Soros and Cecile Wright, BBC producers, thanks for all your hard work to make the series a reality. It was a pleasure working with the BBC team and the other participants. Cynthia Crosers, our 'fixer' in Jamaica, thank you too for your research work and ushering us into the hallowed areas of the Registrar General's Department in Jamaica. The D.N.A. test results inspired our family journey back to Zanzibar in 2009.

Thanks to Joel Stuart for your art work and for understanding the concept behind this project from the beginning. Thanks also for your support when I was forced to stop the work for years due to ill-health. Thanks to Lola Guillamon Garcia for your help and encouragement. To friends, family and colleagues who read and responded to the work over the years, I thank you.

Thanks to my cover designer Evelyn Frazer for your meticulous, exquisite work and the layout. Our meeting was miraculous. Finally, thanks to my photographer, Rebecca May Geddes for author's photograph.

'It seem to me you miss something very important when you cannot read'.
Ambrosine Leteria Brown, 1903-2003

'Man, know thyself'. Gersham Elkanah Brown, 1930-1991

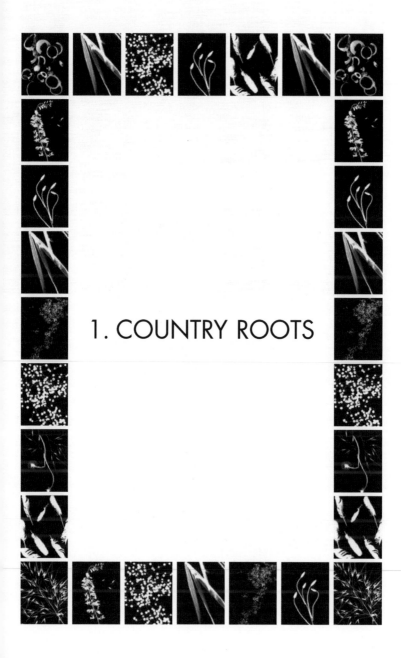

1. COUNTRY ROOTS

Granny's water jar

Glazed Spanish jar, wedged in the ship's hold
Filled with wine for the Govenor's table.
From Corũna to Kingston

A gift from Spanish vineyards
Glazed Spanish jar emptied of wine
Filled with water
From the Negro river

Bare feet swiftly mount the steep river bank
Steady hands balance pails on heads and pour
the life liquid into Granny's water jar.
Glazed Spanish jar, emptied of wine
Filled with water
By this daily family miracle.

Silent sentinel
Providing daily revival
In tropical torpor.
Cracked Spanish jar, emptied of wine
Emptied of water
Filled with memories of a thousand journeys
From Corũna to Kingston
Riverside to outside kitchen
Kitchen to canvas.
Glazed Spanish jar
Granny's water jar.

River Laughter

Perched on a huge boulder in the middle of the river,
Skirt bundled to my thighs,
I sit, captivated by the gushing
of the Negro River.
My mother Iciline,
my father Gersham and their families
all came to this river

To fetch water

      To wash

         To swim

            Io hide

               To bathe ...

...to listen to the music of the Negro river
Each one sat on a stone, abandoned soiled clothes and corn
stick on the bank
Watched the crystal clear water
Felt the blast of the afternoon sun
Dangled feet in the icy depths
Interrupted the relentless roaring of the Negro River
Today my son frolics in the water

Throwing stones

     Splashing

       Racing

         Chasing his cousin,

Their voices, harmonising with the gurgling of the river,

The laughter
Of the Negro River.

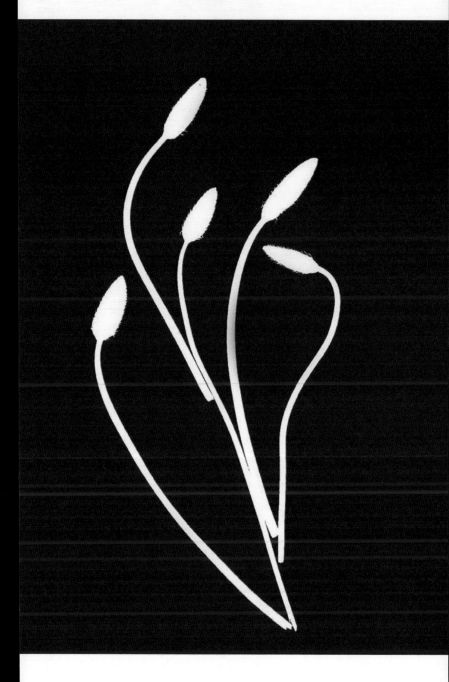

Dance Granny, Dance

Slow rhythmic steps
Beating time to a different drum...
when Quadrille was king

Jane and Louisa will soon come home....

Dance Granny, dance
Miss Ambro's brittle legs, like slender bamboo sticks
Catch every step
Her eyes ablaze,
Her mouth an origami of toothless smiles.
She is vibrant,
Lost in the sheer abandon of remembered joy

Soon come home...
Soon come home...

The music ignites a memory of swirling skirts,
Dignity, daintiness and grace.
'Fingle yu foot man, fingle yu foot'
Straight backs
Careful handling.

Jane and Louisa will soon come home
Into this beautiful garden.

Mr Phillip

For Phillip Brown, 1896-1987

Every night Ambrosine lit the lamp
Home sweet home.
The flame flickered,
Casting long, dancing shadows on the wall.
Long legged spiders scampered to the soot blackened ceiling

Phillip Brown prayed out loud, naming every child, even Clifton.
Gone in 1965
Promised to return to drive his mother in a fish tail car
Over 20 years. Not a word
"Thank you Lord for my friends and my enemies. Bless them all.
Thank you for the coffee crop, the sugar cane, bananas and
plantain.
Thank you for my mule Joe. He's stubborn, Lord but strong.
Thank you Lord. I thank you in Jesus' name. Amen"

Almost 70 years together. Seven children,
Years away in Panama and Cuba.
Together in sickness and health. Till death…
Ambrosine glanced at her atlas man, shrunken in body now
He had towered over her, protecting her, providing for her,
the children and Mamie, her mother, until the end.

…How he beamed at her when she won the cups for quadrille.
On their wedding day he whispered, "Ambrosine, you are a
pretty chile"

"Yes Mr Phillip"…

...Hurricanes and hard times.
"Ambrosine, dinner ready?"
"You have mi water?"
"Please tie mi tie"
"Cream mi face for me,nuh?"
"I look alright?"
Each meal meekly brought
Each river washed garment, starched and ironed.
Seams to slice any fly.

"Yes, Mr Phillip"

That night Mr Phillip lay strangely still
'Yu feeling any pain?'
He shook his head
Eyes alight with visions of glory
"I hear the heavenly music but I cannot speak the language"
Ambrosine's head bowed
She wiped away slow tears.
"When I'm gone, cry,
but don't bawl. You hear Ambrosine?"

'Yes , Mr Phillip'

The lamp light blew out.

Granny, on my Mother's bed

Granny died on my Mother's bed

Closed her eyes
Straightened up
And woke up in glory.

She never returned to her own bed in Trinityville.
Never laid her bony fingers on the starched pillowcases
Never brushed imaginary lint off
the hand embroidered masterpieces from
Panama and Cuba.
Instead, she drifted peacefully into eternity
Under my Mother's loving, watchful gaze.
'You gone and leave me , Granny?'
In a gentle breath, she was gone.
Released from the 99 patchwork years of

Digging yam hills,
Bearing children
Dancing quadrille
Keeping silent,

And ushered into the very presence of her Maker.

'Welcome, Ambrosine
Take your eternal rest.

2. MOTHERHOOD

My Mother's bed

My Mother's bed is an inviting sanctuary,
Always ready to receive me.
On that bed I recline and share tales of battles lost
And won
Of friendship and faith.
My Mother could only look at her Mother's bed,
Wistfully longing to sink into the hand embroidered
masterpieces from Panama and Cuba.
'Who touch mi bed?'
Not a finger could disturb the crisp, perfumed haven
Of Granny's bed.
'Pickney, don't mek me catch you on that bed!'
This morning my son tumbled into my bed
'Good morning Mom'
My bed has none of the mystery and magic of Granny's bed.
Like my Mother's bed, it's a trampoline.
'Don't jump on my bed, child!'
But it's also an inviting sanctuary
ready to receive my child,

There is no other bed...

Like your Mother's bed.

Sunday Smuggling

Sunday at 38
A time for Sunday School and
The Sunday feast.
Roast beef (no mad cows roamed free) Yorkshire pudding,
Carrot juice, rice and peas, trifle and fruit cocktail.
At 36, the menu was standard.

Soup.

We heard Darren's sad tale of King Edwards
floating in a watery moat and wept.
This called for Sunday smuggling
The cargo was human.
Darren leaped over the fence and into our house.
Silence and secrecy were the watch words.
One opened the back door.
One watched the stairs
Another shared food, careful to fill in new holes
In the rice pot.
The carrot juice and the rice and peas quickly converted Darren
and he became a true believer in
Jamaican cuisine
The weekly episode ended with the quiet covering
Of the pots.
The rinsing of evidence
And Darren's hushed departure.

For years he was part of our
Sunday smuggling.

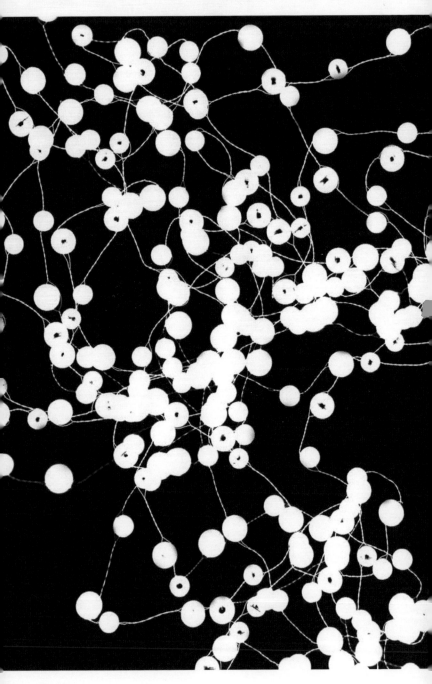

Sheep love

Rushed and rattled
Squeezing,

Stirring

Slicing

A child steps into the dizzy swirl, approaching the vortex
He pulls my hem.
Who is this miniature impediment to my squeezing,

Stirring

Slicing

Sifting

and Sweeping.

'Mummy'…he says
A small coil of rage spirals up inside me
'Didn't I feed you, bathe you, wipe your nose,
your hands, your face, your bottom..
Don't you know that I have to do the

Squeezing,

Stirring

Slicing

Sifting

Scraping

Plus the pressing and packing.
The gentle tug of my hem releases the rage, I exhale.
'I love you, Mummy'
'I love you too ,son'
'I love you… like the sheep… love Jesus'

Circles of Grace

For Tarshem Rai

White tear stained veils shroud sombre faces.
Heads bowed in a Job like silence
Seven days of listening,

> *and shared weeping.*

In the changing circles of grace
Mother's lament is a rising pitch of grief.
Each note, a remembered agony,
Bursting into a crescendo of wailing.

Circles of grace,

Soothing the razor rawness

> *of her sudden loss.*

'My son, my son!'

At the races

Mom, the time keeper, leaps out of bed
Late.

'Hurry up!'

Nothing speeds up this slow, sleepy child

He doesn't snap
Crackle
And pop into action
'Hurry up!'

No time for hands to become airplanes
And dive into the soapy ocean.

'Hurry up!'

Traffic is building with every second
A mile long snake inches up the mountain road

Late

'Hurry up!'

This 6 year old boy turns to face me
Eyes steady
Voice low and direct

'Mummy, I am not a horse
every morning this giddy–up, giddy up

I don't like it!'
Pressure builds with every second of silence
An explosion of laughter .
I apologise
For leading my child into a race he wasn't ready for

We're late
Last past the post
I had missed the starter's orders!

One tear

One wave
Smiles aplenty
Hikes and hills beckoned
'Bye Mom'

From nowhere
One sob filled my chest
Expanding with thoughts of
Every goodbye
Past
and future
'Bye son'

One tear escaped
Trickled slowly

Down

My

Cheek

The boy man was gone.

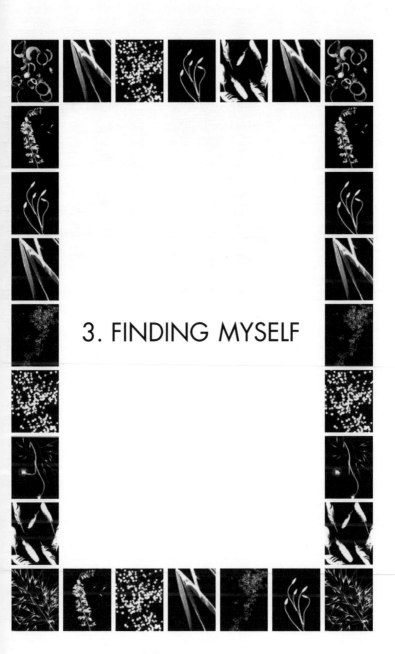

3. FINDING MYSELF

Finger in the dyke

For years
I kept my finger in the dyke
Bravely battling the floods
The tidal waves of disaster which tore through our lives

I kept my finger in the dyke and struggled to salvage human debris

Whispering hope

> *Soothing pain*

> > *Lighting candles of understanding*

> > > *Being there*

Keeping my finger in the dyke.

Now I'm drenched and dishevelled
The dyke has crumbled
My finger is broken
The candles have all blown out

What about ME?

Broken vessel

SHatTerED

Lord…like shards of glass Never the same again.
Make me over, God.

Can you?
Would you?
Will you?
Refashion and reform me?
Find use for the BrOkEn PiEceS?

If you can use any thing, Lord

Use me

Fill this broken vessel with your grace and glory.

Forgive you

For Dad's nightly terror

Haunted by hands
Pleading for mercy
Screaming for those he buried alive
Couldn't save them
The blood red river Volga,
Nature's silent witness.

Forgive you?
For the axe head still in his skull
My treasured black prince
Slaughtered
With one blow.
The earth groaned as he fell dead

Forgive you?
For the missiles you fired
Destined to diminish and destroy me
The wire you tried to coil around me.
Didn't know that I was burrowing my way
Underground
Clawing a tunnel beneath your feet,
To be free of you

Forgive myself
For my steps in the dance of death
The barbed boomerangs I threw
Destroying myself

Forgive you?
Through God's power
To smash the chain of hate and revenge
Give myself a chance
Not to become you
So

I choose

To forgive you

Finding myself

I've just found myself

25 years of playing small
Forced into someone else's iron clad mould of me
Beaten into a flattened version of me
Unable to breathe, stretch and expand into the fullness
of the woman I am today.

Years of swallowing an ocean of sadness
Now unable to shed

        a

           single

              tear

Grateful now for every breath
No time or space for self-pity

Time to discover ....ME!!!

I have finally

      Found

        Myself

          At

            76.

Dance with me

The morning sun smiled on the turquoise waters
And
Enticed me
Beguiled me
To shed the cares

         for my contours

And invited me
To dance.

I swirled and turned,
Floated free in this water ballet.
Gasping at my deft and dainty steps
Surging this way
And that
Weightless.

Even the fish shared my ecstasy.
They encircled me
Darted in and out
Dared to come closer

And

    Danced

        With

           Me.

Onion rings

You peeled away at the outer skins
Slowly and carefully placing each ring on the table
And approached the centre.
I looked at my defences, exposed, evident to all.

How did you accomplish this with no sharp knife?

The smell of onions makes me cry.

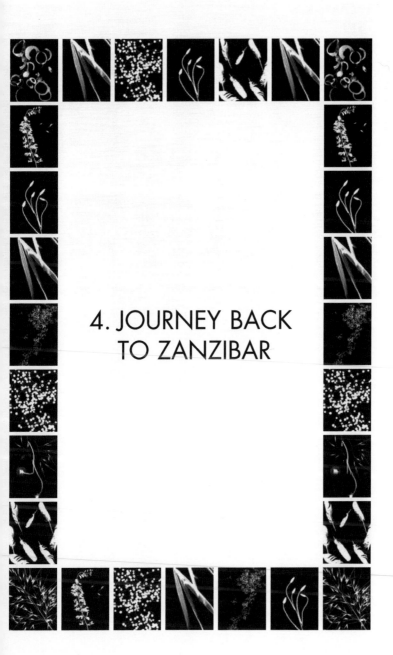

4. JOURNEY BACK TO ZANZIBAR

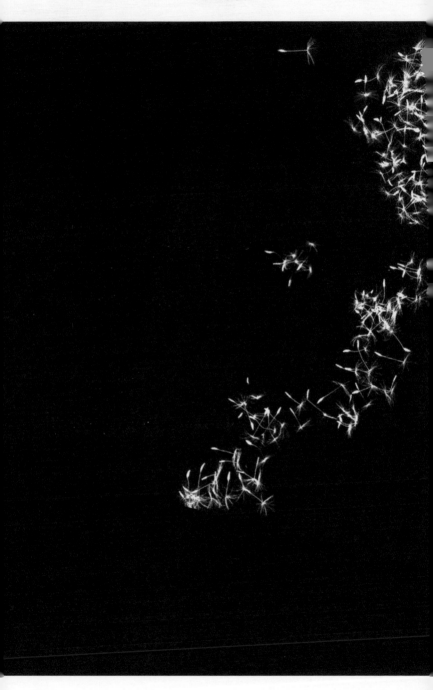

Picture Perfect

Lush green land of Arabian nights
Powder white spit, projects into the sea
Six shades of staggering blue
throbbing with sea life.
The cloud flecked sky kisses the sea,
Picture perfect.

The shark fin sail of the ancient dhow
billows towards the sand,
heaving with chained cargo
The sand drinks the blood, drip...drip...drip...
Stained for three hundred years
The clouds withhold rain in outrage
The dungeon walls scream out

'Nimekua hapa!'

'I was here!'

Zanzibari doorway

Zanzibari doors

The doors declare tales of the past
Mahogany trumpets the triumphs of trade
Teak and Rosewood invite envy and wonder

Each sinuous detail carves out clues to yesteryear
Brass studs shout 'War elephants keep off!'
Flat lintels sneer 'Arabs in town'
Round tops proclaim 'Indians resident'
Craftsmen's skills transform hardwood mass
to delicate flowers and fish,

> lotus,

> cloves

> *...and chains.*

Hopscotch

Roll the stone
Congo
Snatched from the riverside
Marched 6 months through alien land,
Laden and chained.

Roll the stone
Bagamoyo
Laid down my heart,
Pushed past the point of no return into a sea monster.

Roll the stone
Zanzibar
Three dark, dungeon days,
No food, no water
Where is the light?

Roll the stone
Oman

Roll the stone
Liverpool

Roll the stone
Kingston

Roll the stone
Birmingham, Leamington, Kingston, Paris, Leamington

Roll the stone back to Zanzibar.

I don't know my name

Monica who?
I speak English, Jamaican, French and some Spanish
But no Swahili
I don't know my name.

I know Bullring market
Elbowed my way through mountains of shoes
Woke up to the cool, fragrant stillness of a Mandeville morning
Sang beneath the Roselle waterfall
Rafted on the playful blue Rio Grande
Touched gilded bridges on the Seine River cruise
Gasped at the base of the brown Eiffel tour
Licked lavender ice cream on the Promenade Anglaise
Ate fresh turtle soup at Old Harbour bay
Climbed Christophe's Citadelle at Haiti's Le Cap
Sauntered through Kingston, Fort de France, Port au Prince,
Bridgetown, Nassau
 Marseille, Menton
and the Musée Rodin

But I don't know my name.
I don't know the way to my grandmother's village.

Go To Your Mother's Village

Speak to your elders
Listen to their nine night songs
Discover how they thatched their houses
Learn the steps of the quadrille
Boil the Batchelor's button for your sore throat
Repeat the ancient wisdom: 'take sleep mark death'
Go to the cotton tree to see the gold chain
Carry the peeny wallies in jam jars to light the way
Write down your mother's grandmothers' name.

Where is your mother's village?

Journey back to Zanzibar

Snatched from the riverside in the Congo,
Sold for beads and guns,
Marched for nine months to Bagamoyo.
Trudging down, down through the fort
Down, down the sloping, stone steps
to lay down my heart.

Waitu Mukuma batuanyile!
Lord God, have mercy!

Wails of despair as the dhow lurches towards Zanzibar.
Flung in the underground dungeon.
I am buried alive, under the earth,
Stumbling, choking and chained.
The sea is nature's only companion,
Its salty tears setting my wounds on fire.

Waitu Mukuma batuanyile!
Where's the light?...

...No food or water for two days now...
Babies screaming for food and comfort,
Tossed aside as they march me to the market
Where is the light?

Waitu Mukuma batuanyile!

I stumble across the red stream to the market.
The screams of despair throb in my ears and
belly as the sting ray tail claws

                bloody

                      trails

                          through

                              my

                                  back.

Who will flinch first?
"Her. I'll take that one. She didn't cry"

Waitu Mukuma batuanyile!
Lord God, have mercy!

I Will Remember

For my unnamed ancestors

Grandma lulled me to sleep
The same soft chorus wrapped me
around and around like an endless ribbon
She sang as she pounded the millet for our dinner
and smiled as I danced to the rhythm

I remember

Grandma tiptoed to ancient trees
Showed me where they burned iron ore to make steel
Hushed me when I asked her how and why
'Promise you won't tell?'

I remember

Grandma warned me of shadows, spirits and strangers
'Don't wander'
'Write with your right hand'
'If you can't hear, you will feel'

I remember...

...When they snatched me that day from the far river bank
I heard your screams inside my heart
'My spirit will find you!'

I remember

For my mother's tender devotion
I will love
For my father who held me aloft and declared my name
I will triumph
For my brothers and sisters who leapt overboard to escape
caged despair
I will live
I will return, uncoiled and unchained
Free.
For Grandma, whose whispered wisdom guides me still,
I will remember.

Monument to the slaves, Christ Church Cathedral,
Zanzibar. Sculptor, Clara Soros.

45

Welcome sign, Christ Church Cathedral, Zanzibar, site of former slave market.

WELCOME TO
THE ANGLICAN CHRIST CHURCH CATHEDRAL
(THE FORMER SLAVE MARKET SITE)

YOU ARE NOW STANDING AT THE FORMER SLAVE MARKET SITE, THE WORLD'S LAST OPEN SLAVE MARKET AND NOTORIOUS PLACE, WHERE SLAVES FROM EAST AND CENTRAL AFRICA REGIONS WERE BOUGHT AND SOLD.

THE TRADE IN MAN, WOMEN AND CHILDREN WAS STOPPED BY DECREE FROM THE SULTAN OF ZANZIBAR ON 6 JUNE 1873, FOLLOWING THE APPEAL MADE BY Dr. DAVID LIVINGSTONE IN 1857 TO THE MEN OF THE GREAT ENGLISH UNIVERSITIES OF OXFORD AND CAMBRIDGE TO LIBERATE AFRICA FROM SLAVERY.

THE CATHEDRAL CHURCH OF CHRIST WAS BUILT BY BISHOP EDWARD STEERE IN 1874. THE CATHEDRAL STANDS EXACTLY ON THE SITE OF THE FORMER SLAVE MARKET AND THE HIGH ALTAR MARKS THE LOCATION OF THE OLD WHIPPING POST !

PLEASE PURCHASE YOUR TICKET AT THE FRONT GATE TO ENABLE YOU TO EXPLORE MORE ABOUT SLAVERY AND ITS ABOLITION.

ENJOY YOUR TOUR.

Welcome sign, Christ Church Cathedral, Zanzibar, site of former slave market.

47

About the Author

Monica D. Brown was born in Birmingham, UK. She grew up in Royal Leamington Spa, Warwickshire and Jamaica. Monica's first memories of life are of Kingston, Jamaica, hiding behind her mother's skirt. Her life on both sides of the Atlantic has provided her with great opportunities to learn and discover herself. As a teacher, trainer and broadcaster Monica has worked in radio and television. She teaches media production and English. She is also a freelance writer and programme maker. In 2007 she was one of five persons selected by the BBC to explore their family history. The journey took Monica back to Jamaica where she had lived for many years. The D.N.A. test result launched a family journey to Tanzania and Zanzibar in 2009, in search of African roots. This loosely autobiographical collection of poems traces Monica's journey, in part..., back to Zanzibar.

Contact the author at *www.monicabrowntraining.com*

Printed in Great Britain
by Amazon

45139172R00034